The AQI

Acknowledgements

Thanks to the following journals that have kindly published earlier versions of these poems: *Ambit, And Other Poems, Caotang, Magma, Oxford Poetry, Poetry Salzburg Review, The Guardian, The Interpreter's House, The Morning Star, The North, The Rialto, Spittoon, Stand, Strix.*

Earlier versions of some of these poems appeared in *Three Dragon Day* (Smith|Doorstop)

'The Quiz' appeared in *One for the Road* (Smith|Doorstop)
'If you Lived Here You'd be Home by Now' and 'The Blue' appeared in *In Transit: Poems about Travel* (The Emma Press)

Many thanks to The Society of Authors for an Eric Gregory Award in 2015 and to The Wordsworth Trust in 2017 for giving me time and space to write.

Thanks lastly to my family, to my friends and teachers.

For Ed + Michael,

Hope you
enjoy the
poems.
Apologies that
they're a bit
miserable...

Dx

The AQI
David Tait

smith|doorstop

Published 2018 by
Smith|Doorstop books
The Poetry Business
Campo House
54 Campo Lane
Sheffield S1 2EG
www.poetrybusiness.co.uk

Copyright © David Tait 2018

ISBN 978-1-910367-91-9

David Tait hereby asserts his moral right to be identified as the
author of this book.

British Library Cataloguing-in-Publication Data.
A catalogue record for this book is available from the
British Library.

Designed & Typeset by Utter
Printed and bound by CPI Group (UK) Ltd, Croydon, CR0 4YY
Cover image: David Tait
Author photo: Javen Li

Smith|Doorstop Books are represented by and members
of Inpress, www.inpressbooks.co.uk. Distributed by NBN
International, Airport Business Centre, 10 Thornbury Road
Plymouth PL 6 7PP.

The Poetry Business receives financial support from
Arts Council England

Contents

III – *The Popularity of that Sin*

IV – *Lucky Cat*

*Something is always
testing the edges
of the breathable*
– Kay Ryan

I – Three Dragon Day

The Air

A text from the embassy: the air today will not be good.
If possible I should stay indoors.
If possible I should wear a mask.
Today is my day off. I sit and watch

as the air rolls in. The skyscrapers lose their sure angles.
The skyscrapers could almost be whales. I think of Ahab
hurling his pipe. The air buffets against my window.
It is colder inside than outside. The air pants

against the glass. Handprints begin to appear.
Now it's just me. The air mimics the voices of traffic
and hawkers. The traffic and hawkers are drenched in the air.
The walls are starting to sweat.

Beijing Parakeets

Returning again to this hutong hotel
I come in from the frost, remove my mask,
hand over my passport and order a beer.
Check-in will be fifteen minutes, sir.

I step out into the courtyard,
towards the small sad pond, winter water
on the verge of growing its bones,
the slow creak of rusted and muttering carp.

I've already got a pollution headache
but I wait beneath the bare pomegranate tree
and watch the two old parakeets, lovebirds,
huddled up together, one cleaning the feathers
on the others head, the other softly singing.

They've been here every time I've stayed.
I've seen receptionists sneaking them
breakfast-scraps of mango, and watched tourists
smuggling pomegranate's meaty red seeds
between their bars like rubies.

I sip my beer, the birds softly sing,
their little lungs inflating, deflating,
the smog of Beijing simmering around us.

Like this, like this, we go on living,
through the cold and the smog,
through Spring Festival's firecrackers, we go on,
they go on, singing querulous songs:

*O fire lantern, you are floating
through the gathering thunderheads.*

Smog

I don't have long to write
so let me tell you that today's smog
is so thick that I've sat inside
with a headache, wearing a face-mask
next to an air purifier, that the recorded figures
are double the hazardous limit, that these measurements
are probably a generous estimate, that I'm sitting
within my dubious force-field with leaking eyes,
that outside there are mechanics and window cleaners
and school kids and flower-sellers with lungs
like the bottoms of an hour glass,
that they are breathing and coughing
and dying too soon, that I love a man
but they won't let him in, that it kills me,
that it's killing me

The Gobi Desert

All of the readers were wearing facemasks.
Outside: the AQI at hazardous, a Mongolian sandstorm.

They sat in a circle and took turns to read.
Outside the sand chipped away at the glass.

I had another headache. A poet stood and read a poem.
I could hardly hear the words and couldn't read her lips.

I watched her facemask move out and in, in and out,
heard her shout something amidst the gusts of dust.

Then she sat as another stood up. No applause,
I'm not even sure there was language.

Afterwards I asked them why they wore the masks,
that the audience couldn't understand or hear.

One of them laughed and gestured to the window,
well no-one listens anyhow.

The Facemask

I wear it because of the sky,
the sun overhead a filmed eye.

I wear it walking to the metro, respectful
of the wagons' black fumes.

I wear it on the metro, we all do.
We stare at each other like surgeons
during a tricky operation.

I wear it at work. See,
the one correcting grammar on the whiteboard is me.

I start to wear it on dates.
I imagine his slick lips, white rows of teeth.
During sex, we leave more than our socks on.

Sometimes I gasp in the night
and raise a hand to my mouth.

I can feel it starting to replace me.

Three Dragon Day

Forget the science of particulate matter,
air pollution comes from dragons.

On a blue day the dragons are far from the city.
On a day like today the air scratches and growls.

Imagine them, out there, wrapped around skyscrapers,
shrieking to each other through blast furnace throats,

their scales buckled steel, eyes deep as mineshafts,
grey wings rippling with varicose veins.

Putting on a face-mask, a five year old girl
looks out at a city vague as Monet's London.

Today is a three dragon day, she says, then heads out
onto the street, towards the crossing, and is gone.

Red Alert

After a week at Very Unhealthy
we get word that a smog cloud from Inner Mongolia

is making its way south-west. The size of Denmark,
it drifts towards us like a jellyfish

and for one long week it promises to be
the unshiftable sitting-ghost of our lungs.

Schools will call smog playtime,
kids watching Tom & Jerry in face-masked rows,

and cars with even-numbered licence plates will be taken
from the roads. A stand-up comedian will perform a skit

about officials doing nothing until the smog hits them,
starts to pick their pockets. But aunties will still be dancing,

as uncles lash their spinning tops in quietened squares.
And the workers? Workers will work. We'll watch them

from behind our windows, as they appear
then disappear, then appear again, like wraiths.

Temple Built from Bricks of Smog
After Jianguo Xiongdi

Each brick donated by an artist:
the deity rests in a smoking shrine.

We offer old fruit and river water
the only foreigners to have made the trip.

Someone in the prayer hall is coughing his guts up.
A young soldier solders a lock to a tree.

A tour guide points out the roof's iconography:
a dragon, two manticores, the skeletons of buildings

and the usual pilgrim perched on his horse.
It's another day of restricted visibility, but we see him

in greyscale, peering over his ledge,
looking like he's weighing up the fall.

The Blue

I hear her behind me
beautiful, beautiful,
on days like this
when the blue seems endless,
when the train belts south
for hours and hours,
when cooling towers simmer
like contented kettles,
when it's winter, but you see
the twigged nests of trees
and think of life not death,
when the further south you go
the more things go on living,
when in a split-second
you pass a field of peasant farmers
unearthing vegetables and watch one
lift his face towards your train
and imagine him smiling or sighing,
no facemask today, maybe humming
some sonorous peasant song,
one of those you've heard on the metro, at night;
when the sun glints on the pylons
that seem to hold their cables a little looser,
on days like this, where you can race the vapour
trails of planes, when the woman behind you
takes picture after picture, for eight whole hours,
pictures of edgelands, pylons, girders, half-finished
skyscrapers, traffic jams, brown fields, iced-over streams,
construction vehicles, the sky, rubbish bags
on a platform, trees, a hamlet's hillside pagoda,
muttering beautiful, piaoliang, beautiful,
a maple tree, beautiful, a roadside quarry, a glass factory,
the sky, the sun shining on grey stones,

ice floating down the Yangtze, junk boats full of coal,
a school, a tree full of egrets, a lonesome bull, more pylons,
piaoliang, the sky, smoke rising from a bonfire,
an abandoned town, a colourful village, a fishing lake,
shipping crates, a countryside driving school, a JCB
perched on a mound of rocks, a pipeline, a farmhouse,
a white stone hut in a brown field, six hay bales,
beautiful, the blue, beautiful
then a sudden tunnel, her own reflection,
then out again into the blue, it's heavy and astonishing blast,
like bells, bells that have just stopped ringing,
on days like these, days like these
when it feels like we're winning.

II – The House of Frantic Stepping

If You Lived Here You'd be Home by Now

I woke on a bullet train
to find my long-dead mother
had made an investment
in twelve baby sharks
that knifed around our old carp pool.

Outside the train the typhoon raged.
I saw my mother in the hills
telling frantic trees these sharks
would grow into my fame.
Here is her house, they'll say,

The House of Frantic Stepping.
Of course, I tried to talk her down,
but how can you reason with a shade?
My mother glared back at me,
drenched in tradition.

A tunnel for a mile, two miles, then out.
The left window revealed Guangxi's jade foothills,
the right, the gloom of the M25.
My mother fed her sharks our heirlooms by hand.
Trucks hauled our past towards a future.

Nothing

Winter, light snow: and because you've asked for nothing
you've arrived at this hillside monastery, the hour late,

the wind beat-boxing in the hood of your coat. The abbot
takes one look at you and sighs, resting one arm on his radiator,

gesturing the way to the half-frozen pool, where you stare alone
into the black rectangle of water, the surface grizzled with weeds,

the murk of years of turtle-shit, the heavy stink of your own face.
You've asked for nothing, and yet a small deep glimmer of gold

slips into your reflection, then another, then your face ripples
and erupts with murmuring mouths. *They think you're here for them*

says the abbot, somehow beside you, *they think you're for them,*
even though you came here for nothing, for less than nothing.

He shakes his head and throws them a handful of food. *And we are here*
aren't we, doing what they want? The snow becomes heavier.

I'll show you around the abbot says, and he leads you round the grounds;
the deities huddled in their shrines,

the place the monks hid in times of trouble, the statues of great sufferers,
the huge and immovable trees. The abbot tells you stories about each,

then takes you back to the pool. It's frozen solid, snow is settling on the ice.
What happens to the fish beneath the ice? you ask, and the abbot laughs.

What fish are you talking about? You point to the pool, and he laughs.
Nothing lives in that pool but your own thoughts.

The abbot smiles, then laughs, then walks away into the blizzard.
All that's left is this snow rectangle, the swimming thoughts
you must feed.

Learning to Count: A House by Two Rivers in Winter

一　a fencepost collapsed under the weight of snow

二　two bodies were floating downstream

三　and the things between them like a third body

四　we doled out our thoughts like spare blankets

五　a man was hobbling down the narrow lane

六　he stopped for breath at our window

七　he rested his arms on the bridge rail

八　the bodies drifted down different rivers

九　the pylons above him were fizzing with giddiness

十　a crucifix was nailed to a whitewashed wall

String

Last night I dreamed your mother
tied a string around your toes.
I knew her right away, even though

we've never met. I knew her eyes, wide
like yours, and watched her twiddling
the thin white band, her hands

fiddling with your feet as you slept.
In the dream you were not a child.
In the dream you were you as I know you.

Your mother didn't know me at all. She asked
for my help. She made me tauten the string
along your outstretched foot, then bound

each toe, humming. I watched your foot flex
against the ties. I watched her walk through the door.
In the morning you stirred and stared at the string.

"What have you done?" you said.

The Traditional and Virtuous Green Zone

I woke to the explosion of a forty-foot tree
being dropped from a truck to the tarmac.

Twenty more arrived, and I watched as a gang
of workmen banged away at the root soil,

men hacking and spitting with sledgehammers,
then a crane came and settled them in.

By lunchtime cicadas were belting out their songs
and seniors played chess in the shade.

By sunset a man did a roaring trade in singing birds,
and two rival groups of aunties danced to garish music.

A knock at the door announced an official with a leaflet:
You are today living in the traditional and virtuous green zone

an urban orchard with fifty years of harmonious history.
I started to laugh and turned to tell my partner

but sitting in his place, shocked to see me
was a man who looked old, like his father.

Why That Building is Red

Driving between centres in Shenzhen
my colleague points out the sights:

"You see that building? That is where we are going.
It took them just three days to build each floor
which is why we say 'at Shenzhen speed'".

We are driving down the main road in her silver car.
I am flicking through the notes of a class I'll teach later
on brainstorming ideas for a phone app.

"And this place here", she gestures, flailing an arm,
"This is the best place in town for getting copies.
Shenzhen's most renowned forgerers work here."

We stop at some lights by a large red building.
It looks odd set against the chrome high-rises.
"Oh and this building, this red one,

this is where people go if they need to be killed."
I look at it more closely. There are two soldiers lounging
at the entrance, a red banner flapping in the breeze.

"Of course, that doesn't happen as much any more,
just mainly in the old times. The building is red to warn us
against ghosts. Ghosts are unlucky for business."

The lights change and we leave it behind. It lessens
to the size of a brick, then a smudge. "And here" she says,
slowing the car, "Here is our Starbucks."

Post Truth

A week of autumn snow, and today the sun,
the buildings fizzy with melting, the beggar
draping his sheets over the bank's homeless-spikes.

My daughter runs under the sycamore trees,
shouts *look it's still snowing, it's still snowing,*
clumps of old snow falling around her.

Who am I to deny her her truth?
I stand watching as she picks up a handful of mush,
that evaporates as she throws it towards me.

She's eight now, audacious in her red sweater.
How could I deny her? This week's been good
for the both of us, it seems; but today the trees

are shedding their magic white skins.
Look at my daughter, spinning in her small world of snow.
Now tell me, why would I make her up?

Two Vans

Ayi is going for her ultrasound
in the white van on the outskirts.

She's been throwing up in the closet
each morning for a week.

"It's that bug that's going around"
is what she tells the boss.

If it's a boy she will hand in her notice.
If it's a girl she will schedule another appointment

with the man who drives the black van.
Last time she stuck the photo to the ceiling

and stared and stared at it, until her eyes blurred,
and it dissolved, and was gone.

An Escalator into the Rain

We stand at the bottom of the stairwell
and look up at the storm; raucous lightning
lighting the others. I am among the luckless,
the umbrella-less.

How long have I stood here?
People in bright raincoats take out plastic wallets
and deposit their phones. They board the escalator
like celebrities about to face the paparazzi.

Such storms here, and there's no letting up.
I watch one of the others make a dash for it,
the water is bouncing down the stairs,
the thunder booms. He's gone

and I must go too. I step onto the conveyor
and lift my backpack above my head.
I'm reminded for a moment of boarding a plane,
of knowing there is no way back.

Window Cleaners

They stand on the tops of skyscrapers
like toy soldiers, they of the pole-system,
the lowering box.

Today they are abseiling down Huaxia Plaza,
one hundred floors of prime location
and not a unit of it let.

I imagine them as deep-sea gravediggers,
as tiny fish that nibble the flesh between toes,
blind masseurs tasked with a sperm whale,

or just as they are: men on thin winches,
pummelling their feet against the bomb-proof glass,
washing away footprints as they drop.

Next to them another building is going up,
cranes lifting girders, planks of wood.
As night falls we see sparks fall from high floors

and the window cleaners pause a moment, look up
at the new biggest building, a hundred and ten floors
of prime location and, so far, none of it let.

Lunch Poem

The construction workers have lunch at noon.
They unplug their circular saws, put down their sledgehammers
and head to the nearby park.

It's then that the Guangzhou Treetop Orchestra of Cicadas
launches into its great insecty opus:
GET UP!   BUILD!   CREATE!

无辜

A message on We-Chat. One of the villagers
has lost it. He's climbed to the top of the old pagoda
and unfurled a banner: Innocent.

A crowd has gathered, munching cucumbers.
They speculate how he made it through the thick
barbed wire. The police arrive, plug in a loudspeaker

and try to coax him down. *What is he innocent of?*
we ask, *Uncle*, the police shout, *Uncle come down.*
The villager grips on to his banner. The sun slinks

behind the pagoda. People are beginning to leave.
The police keep asking to look at my passport.
They keep checking my phone for a camera.

The villager stayed up there for almost three days.
As the sun set he suddenly lifted his head
and screamed, *Innocent! Innocent! I'm innocent!*

then jumped.

The police stood around a while after he'd hit.
They made quiet notes and shook their heads.
They carried him off. They folded up the banner.

混混

The migrant worker has a grievance.
He is writing it down on the flagstones
of Tiyu Xilu, ideograph by ideograph

using different sticks of coloured chalk
and a single slab for each character.
I can't read much but I know good writing.

I recognise "no" and "trouble" and "person" and "can't".
The other passers-by pause a little
then move on, glancing over their shoulders,

shepherding away their children.
Someone taps him lightly on the back.
"They are coming your way", they say.

The migrant worker shakes his head and laughs.
He looks left and right for their light blue tunics.
They are approaching him from every direction.

Dongshankou

Sometimes it's enough to come
to the café from the guidebook

and order coffee, an afternoon to marinade
in the pale sunlight, flicking through Szymborska

and copies of the architectural periodicals
the owner happens to stock.

I'm not an architect. I will probably never own a house,
but who is to know in this city, where my tongue

can't negotiate even simple consonants,
where the coffee I've ordered arrives as tea,

where the door opposite me suddenly widens a crack
and a stranger takes my picture.

The Dutch Masters

Hal Robson Kanu scored last night's winner
and with a similar turn and drop of the shoulder
you could shimmy down an alley to here:

Dafen, Shenzhen: world capital of the knock-off,
alleys filled with Rembrandts, Matisses and Klimts,
hundreds of artists, sat with their thermoses

of Oolong, their little transistor radios.
I've already turned down two portraits of Mao
and a painting of lychees, plush on their boughs.

I chat with a guy painting The Grand Bazaar
and he says, with a shrug, oh that's what it is,
that he's not really bothered about Istanbul

but there's been a recent demand, and it pays.
A couple of months back it was Bavarian castles
for a German pub chain expanding in Brazil.

He says the work doesn't thrill him, but he's good
at it, that it pays. What would you rather paint?
I ask, and he laughs, and says The Dutch Masters

but their pictures don't pay. He shows me a binder:
De Boer, Bergkamp, Overmars, and towards the back
Johan Cruyff, dropping his shoulder, leaving the defenders for dead.

Writing Class, Guangzhou

I ask them to bring in a thing
that they care for. They bring:

a hairpin carved in the shape
of a carp; a policeman's flask;

young elephants engulfed
by their mother's trunk, a statue;

a picture of a rabbit, the only toy
they left her after joining school.

One lady has brought in her husband.
He sits in the corner sipping lemon tea.

The others: a silver coin that dates
from the Qing dynasty; a string of pearls

that survived The Great Leap Forward;
the only remaining photo of a family.

She remembers the day it was taken,
her sister crying and not keeping still,

the hesitation she felt looking into the lens,
her father's hands gripping her shoulders.

A History of the World in Forty Walls

A biting Autumn day.
The cable car lifts me up from grey Beijing
and drops me here,
with sky we haven't had in months,
with three hours to walk where I want.
I undo my facemask and take it in.

It was built as a defence against northern barbarians
and stretches for over six thousand kilometers.
It's the only wall in the world that really matters ...

But what about the other walls?
The West Wall of Jerusalem,
the walls of Constantinople, Dubrovnik,
the West Bank Barrier?
What about fallen walls: Berlin, Jericho, Hadrian's,
the wall in Belfast they called the Peace Line,
the crumbling wall of Western Sahara?

And then there's Phnom Penh, York, Ayuthaya.

Or those joking walls: the sticky gum wall of Seattle
and Kamphaeng Phet (the diamond wall) with its looted
Buddhas.

We climb The Great Wall
with our manic cameras
and I'm thinking of something humbler:
the wall my mother pressed a glass to
in our rough end terrace,
the wall we played football against,
the wall by the river
and its hidden footholds
and the day it let me fall.

Childhood walls: the truants' wall,
the redbrick walls of Woodhouse Ridge
the pebbledashed paper-round estate walls,
dry stone walls, the ruined dam near Helvellyn
we called Jean-Claude.

The snowline,
which was a kind of wall,
the cairn that marked out
Swirrel Edge, little shelters
that dotted high fells,
the crying walls of Guangzhou in the spring
and the walls of the knackered slum
covered in slogans
and the people still living there regardless, holding out
for a better deal
as new walls rose around them.

Super expressways,
which are another wall.

High speed rail links, the people who had to
up and leave,
the cataract of smog between here and Hong Kong.

Ramparts
barricades
markers
territories
border crossings
trade zones

Good walls make good neighbors.

Why don't they go back to where they came from?

A house with love has elastic walls.

If you press a spring too hard
it will snap back. You must always remember this.

And this:
We grope along the wall like blind men,
We grope like those who have no eyes;
We stumble at midday as in the twilight,
Among those who are vigorous we are like dead men.

III – The Popularity of that Sin

Beijing after Tianjin

i

The morning after the explosions,
Central office, the visa officer
has been in the bathroom vomiting twenty minutes,
We-Chat is full of pictures and videos
and the net is going slow, not fast enough
to conference call. My colleague asks
if I've brought my umbrella, even though
Beijing is arid with dust, I say I've not
well bring it tomorrow she says I say I will.
VPN will not connect, BBC is blocked, local
television is not covering the explosions
that were so large they could be seen from space.
The day wears on and one by one the pictures
and videos disappear.

ii

Teachers meeting: we brainstorm ideas
for a new class and go through the month's data.
In the break we talk about yesterday
and one says how one of his students was crying
and another said her family live near there
but were safe, she broke down when she said it
and the other students didn't look at her
and shuffled their feet so she left and sat in The Lounge.
After the meeting I go for a walk down to the CCTV building.
Take your umbrella, my colleague says, you don't know
what might be in the rain. I check the AQI: yellow.
Huge crowds.

iii

The course has been cancelled.
East Beijing has been shut down.
The army need Line One, The Forbidden City,
Tiananmen Square and the CBD to practice.
My hotel tells me there will be a curfew.
I must be home by 8pm tonight, tomorrow, the night
after that, they'll let me know if this changes.
It's a war parade to celebrate peace. North Korea
exchanges fire with South Korea. A CNN report
from Tianjin goes viral. The reporter starts his report
then gets surrounded by a crowd who shout
Tianjin is for China! Chinese problems are China's business!
They beat him. CNN releases a statement and is criticised.
Later that day another statement stating these people
were distressed relatives. Videos and links disappear.
People I respect post things like 'America tells lies about us!'
My colleague calls to tell me she has good news:
a new venue has been arranged. Clouds appear,
the sky darkens, but it does not rain.

iv

Qing Dynasty restaurant: open courtyard,
a couple of bedraggled mynah birds who imitate R2D2.
Wifi still slow, still no VPN, Guardian and BBC not connecting
due to network issues. Factories closing ahead of the parade,
further rumors of acid rain. The TV is full of feel good stories.
Last night a Frenchman and his new Chinese bride exited the Uniqlo
in Sanlitun and were stabbed and stabbed by a man with a sabre
who screamed I hate America as he stabbed. No one intervened
but some people screamed and a number of people filmed
the whole thing, their videos starting before the stabbing started.
It didn't make the news. The news is full of old men talking about
how they overthrew the Japanese aggressors. Later someone suggests

that the Frenchman stole that man's woman. This is the only logical
reason such a reaction could have been provoked. I stab a piece
of bean curd and listen to the mynahs. On the way home I feel stares
on my neck. That night it rains and rains.

v

The morning of the course: sky blue as Tasmania,
I walk the short journey to Dongsi metro, past the police blockade.
A man is whipping a metal spinning top, old women are dancing.
Overhead warplanes are orbiting the city.
Down the road Mo Farah and Usain Bolt are warming up
for their races. We-Chat is full of pictures mocking Kim Jong-Un
and a story that the Tianjin blast site will be turned into an eco-park.
The VPN connects. The man with the sabre has been captured.
Overhead the helicopters form a 70 in the sky. The metro
is full of black and white footage from The War of Japanese Aggression.
I get scanned three times. My passport is checked twice.
My water is confiscated.
I get to the office and my colleague says how lucky we are,
the sky is so blue, what wonderful weather to celebrate peace.
I smile and I say yes we are lucky,
I say it's as though they'd had it planned.

The Quiz

I know I've been reading too much news
when walking to the quiz, beneath the neon lights of
a body massage parlour I read the words 'bloody massacre'
and when I stop to look again, then again, my mind does
this thing where it checks and double checks itself

and thinks 'isn't the word "of" weird, surely "of" shouldn't
be spelt like that', and before I can think there's two men
walking past speaking English, of all languages, something
about a camel, which happens to be where this quiz is,
The Camel, an ex-pat pub near Fuxing Lu, a quiz host called Ned.

Is there are a sturdier name than Ned? A pint or two
then I look for the loo, the toilet – 'to let' – but this one makes sense.
I come back to my table to this question: 'Rank the following incidents
from the most people killed to the least people killed:
The Utoya Shootings, Dunblane, The Nanoor Massacre,
The Passover Massacre. Four points available.'

We get it right and we cheer. I walk back past
the Bloody Massage parlor listening to a man telling his girlfriend
"well at least he says what we're all thinking. It's about time
we had a man in charge who wasn't..." but he's drowned out
by one of those lumbering road-clean trucks, spraying the road
with water playing the same warning tune in every city I've been:

it's a small world after all
it's a small world after all
it's a small world after all
it's a small   small   world

White Lamborghini in a Disabled Parking Space

I don't think it's possible, but I'll tell you what I saw.
I saw the parking attendant pocket his pad,
calmly tuck his pen behind his ear
then slam a great red brick through its windscreen.
I saw a crowd gather as he pulled a crowbar
from the air and went to work on the wheels.

It sounds off the rails, but I was there, I saw.
I saw the whole thing, the roaring traffic attendant
building up a sweat, the gobsmacked crowd
filming it on phones, the street-cleaners struggling
to keep straight faces, the CCTV cameras
swivelling from the proof of the scene.

I know it was all probably a dream
but I saw the owner come back. I saw the traffic attendant
walk away whistling, I saw the crowds disperse
whilst humming a tune. I walked past a busker
who'd given it words and sang it through a shower of coins.
I can't remember how the tune went, but he'd called it The Cost of Living.

On the Weakening of Angels

This one is for those of you
not yet at the mercy of hate.

Know that if today you are loved
that love can be taken

easily as a tap on the shoulder,
a whispered kiss. Know it will be reasonable,

as reasonable and astonishing as this autumn flare
of gingko leaves, these bloodening maples.

Know too that some will hand themselves over,
casual as a coat for a cloakroom,

will take their ticket with both hands
for whatever waits in the silent theatre.

Know, finally, that the angels are losing
their brightness, that they have protected you

yes, protected you, as nobly as your white blood cells,
God-fearing country, that has chosen the devil.

The Fake News Colossus

Listen folks, America has never wanted the tired or poor

nor the huddlers who think breath comes for free.

Look at me: a self-made man.

We all agree and have voted on this.

Folks, if you've washed up lost, tempest-tost you're lucky.

Now go through this door and shut up.

Ask yourself, would you let you in?

After Orlando

Antonio: *Fie, fie!*
Salarino: *Not in love, neither? Then let us say you are sad.*

✳

The day the act passed
we didn't get married
we went dancing
we didn't go to the usual
we went to the new bar
cheap drinks, I slipped
my arm around his waist
we kissed but then a man came
put his face against mine
shouted why can't you go
to your own fucking bar
and I said this is our bar
as much as it's yours and he said
fuck you you fucking sick faggot
and his friend dragged him off
and said sorry I'm sorry he's just drunk
and I said he really should be sorry
and she said look he's just drunk, let it go,
and anyway why did you have to provoke him
and I said how did I provoke him
and she said you know very well
and I turned around and my friend
had run out into the night.

✳

Two weeks into his recovery
we played board games: Scrabble,
Boggle, Monopoly. He needed rest

so we never finished. Then we played
Guess Who? but instead of asking
about blonde hair, gender or glasses
we asked would you fuck this person, would
this person kick a tramp, is this person
a good person do you think and he'd laugh
for a bit and his bruises would shimmer.

✳

During the attack I was sat in a Shanghai theater
listening to Ian McKellen as he talked about Shakespeare,
about Antonio from *The Merchant of Venice*: gay, lovelorn,
and the directors who'd approached him to play the part,
and their revulsion when Ian told them Antonio was gay
and they said no, so he said no, and there was an ovation,
clap clap clap clap clap clap clap clap clap clap clap
and suddenly a buzz in my pocket and I stopped clapping
and looked, a BBC news alert, a shooting, another shooting.

✳

The DJ was playing a typical set that incorporated
what we thought was gunshots as part of the music
Four shots, pop pop pop pop

✳

Would you let him suck you off?
Ha, let's see … probably not
Clack clack clack
Well, would you let him buy you a drink?
Well, what kind of drink?
Any kind of drink you wanted.
Hmm ha, I'm struggling to picture this person
actually buying me a drink. Clack clack clack.
So he looks stingy? Stingy? *Conservative with money.*

53

Hmm... not really. Maybe a bit shy.
Anyway, who said anything about he. I'd let her
buy me a mojito, but I doubt she'd want to.

✳

Why did you run off like that?
I'm sorry, I just... I dunno, I panicked.
You panicked? I panicked. I'm sorry.
I'm sorry I left you there alone. You're sorry?
Yes, I'm sorry I left you there alone. Do you
want to go to another place. Another place?
Yeah, like, maybe the usual place. A gay bar?

✳

Ian McKellen is asking the audience to name
all of Shakespeares plays. The audience are screaming
Gentlemen of Verona, Merry Wives of Windsor
people look down at their phones, up, down, up,
down at their phones. *The Merchant of Venice!*
The Merchant of Venice!

✳

A gay bar?
Yes, I know. I just want to be safe.
Safe?
Yes safe. I just want to be safe with you.

✳

Mommy I love you. In club they shooting
U ok?
Trapp in bathroom
What club?
Pulse. Downtown. Call police.

*

Okay, so, next question does this person like gays?
I think this person says that they don't mind gays.
Interesting. Well, we've already established
that Bernard here is outwardly a massive homophobe. Clack.
I would say this person definitely has some prejudice
but they hide it well, they have a gay black friend or something.
Okay, got it. Hmm... would this person
vote for the Tories? Oh God, definitely!
Clack clack clack clack

*

Are you and your mate gay?
Of course, this is a gay bar. Aren't you?
No mate, I'm not. But don't get me wrong
I've got nothing against you gay people.
Well, what a fucking relief.
No need to be like that mate.
Like what?
I'm just trying to be nice.
Thanks, but please leave me alone.
Will do mate, wouldn't let you near me anyway.
Backs to the wall lads.
Backs to the wall.

*

In other political news today
a nominee running for the presidency of Ghana
wants to have gays put to death by firing squad.
George Boateng says it is time to eradicate homosexuality.
There is too much indiscipline in Ghana, he told Kasapa radio.
Under my presidency when a corrupt person, or gay or lesbian
are arrested, the law will make it possible for the courts

55

to sentence the offender to death by firing squad.
It will be a public event, to be witnessed by all to serve as a deterrent.

＊

Backs to the wall lads.
Backs to the wall.

＊

Would this person ever consider running for the Ghanaian
presidency?
Ha, almost certainly.
Clack clack clack

＊

I'm gonna die
I'm calling them now;
U still in there;
answer our damn phone;
call them; call me

＊

"He said 'please don't text' –
that's the exact words he used 'please don't text'"

＊

Call them mommy. Now.
He's coming. I'm gonna die.
Is anyone hurt? What bathroom is he in?
Lots yes.
Are you with police. Text me please.
No. Still here in bathroom. He has us. They need to come get us.

✳

Does this person look cute?
Cute?
Yeah, you know cute.
You know, I honestly can't tell anymore.
Really? That's not like you.
I know. I'm feeling tired. Can we stop playing for a while?
Of course.
David, can we talk?
Of course. What would you like to talk about?

✳

Is the man in the bathroom wit u?
He's a terror.
Yes.

✳

I thought he was into me.
That song was playing and I'd had
I'd had too much to drink
and he came over and whispered
did I want, did I want to
go outside with him, so I nodded
and he smiled and said follow me
and I smiled and said okay and followed
like a fucking idiot I followed

✳

Mark you this, Bassanio,
The devil can cite scripture for his purpose.

57

＊

Martin Benitez Torres, 33
Jonathan Antonio Camuy Vega, 24
Juan P Rivera Velazquez, 37
Luis S. Vielma, 22
Frank Jimmy Dejesus Velazquez, 50
Luis Daniel Wilson-Leon, 37
Jerald Arthur Wright, 31

＊

Backs to the wall, lads.
Backs to the wall.

＊

Stanley Almodavar III, 23
Oscar A Aracena-Montero, 26
Amanda Alvear, 25
Rodolfo Ayala-Ayala 33
Antonio Davon Brown, 29
Darryl Roman Burt II, 29
Angel L Candelario-Padro, 28

＊

Pastor Roger Jiminez of Sacramento's Very Baptist Church
Praised the Orlando shooter and lamented that:
"the tragedy is more of them didn't die. I'm kind of upset
he didn't finish the job." The pastor also said that the killings
had made Orlando safer, and added his preference would be
to line LGBTQ people up against a wall for a firing squad to
"blow their brains out". YouTube removed the video of Jiminez's sermon,
citing its policy against hate speech. Jiminez later told a Sacramento report
that his sermon was not meant to incite violence against LGBT people.
"All I'm saying is that when people die who deserve to die,
　　　　　　　　　　　　　　it's not a tragedy" he said.

58

＊

You're not a fucking idiot for following.
You're not. Listen to me.
How were you to know what would happen?
Of course it was going to happen. It's been happening.
It's been happening and happening my whole life.
It will happen my whole life.

＊

Juan Chevez-Martinez, 25
Luis Daniel Conde, 39
Cory James Connell, 21
Tevin Eugene Crosby, 25
Deonka Deidra Drayton, 32
Simon Adrian Carrillo Fernandez, 31
Leroy Valentin Fernandez, 25

＊

It wasn't your fault.
I know.
Look at me. It wasn't your fault.
I know. I. You're right. It wasn't my fault.
It wasn't my fault. I know.

＊

Mercedez Marisol Flores, 26
Peter O. Gonzalez-Cruz, 22
Juan Ramon Guerrero, 22
Paul Terrell Henry, 41
Frank Hernandez, 27
Miguel Angel Honorato, 30
Javier Jorge-Reyes, 40

A tweet from Donald Trump:
Appreciate the congrats for being right on radical Islamic terrorism.
I don't want congrats, I want toughness & vigilance. We must be smart!.

Jason Benjamin Josaphat, 19
Eddie Jamoldroy Justice, 30
Anthony Luis Laureanodisla, 25
Christopher Andrew Leinonen, 32
Alejandro Barrios Martinez, 21
Brenda Lee Marquez McCool, 49
Gilberto Ramon Silva Menendez, 25

know not why I am so sad.
It wearies me; you say it wearies you.

Kimberley Morris, 37
Akyra Monet Murray, 18
Luis Omar Ocasio-Capo, 20
Geraldo A Ortiz-Jiminez, 25
Erik Ivan Ortiz-Rivera, 36
Joel Rayon Paniagua, 32
Jean Carlos Mendez Perez, 35

The thing is. Can I tell you this, David?
The thing is, after he'd finished
when every part of me hurt
I mean every single part
and he was looking at me with

this half-disgust half-shame
I asked him how he could do this
to another person
and do you know what he said
he said, he said, you are not
you are not a fucking person
and he spat at my feet.

✳

Enrique L. Rios, Jr, 25
Jean C. Nives Rodriguez, 27
Xavier Emmanuel Serrano Rosado, 35
Christopher Joseph Sanfeliz, 24
Yilmary Rodriguez Solivan, 24
Edward Sotomayor Jr, 34.
Shane Evan Tomlinson, 33

✳

This is one of the worst atrocities committed against LGBT people
in the western world for generations, and it has to be called out.

*Well, it's something that's carried out against human beings isn't it,
no matter what their ...*

✳

He said, he said, you are not
you are not a fucking person
and he spat and he spat
at my feet

✳

No! No ... this has to be called out for what it is; this was
an intentional attack on LGBT people

I don't think that you have ownership of horror of this crime
because you're gay.

Can I just say I find this astonishing?

I'm not Jewish, and I'm not gay, and I'm not French, but I'm still
equally horrified by these crimes...

✳

The Spectator:

'the reliably idiotic left-wing columnist Owen Jones
had a temper tantrum while reviewing the papers
on Sky News ... apparently because neither the presenter
or the other reviewer would accept that the tragedy
was all about Owen. The only thing that mattered
was that it was an attack upon gay people, and so it was
a kind of singularity, an atrocity which Owen, being gay,
could have to himself.'

✳

In sooth, I know not why I am so sad.
It wearies me; you say it wearies you.

✳

Why do you think gay people are so angry about
Orlando being called an Islamic attack. Why are they so dramatic?

They aren't being dramatic, there's a long history of homophobia,
and not mentioning that the gunman specifically targeted gay people
is a kind of homophobic erasure. Homophobia still exists.

When will the gay community stop complaining? You can get married,
you can adopt. We have let you be like us.

You see, that's the thing. You think you've let us be like you. You
think it's okay to give us permission.

✳

Another article: 'Owen Jones flounces off Sky News set.'

Flounces.

✳

Would she help me if I needed money?
Would he stand up for me in a fight?
If she owned a hotel would she let us share a room?
Would she mutter about it to her friends?
Would he march for me? In another age would he turn me in?
Would she come dancing and say I'm alright?
Would she ignore me if I came up to her, bleeding?
Would she cry if I read her The Man with Night Sweats?
Do you think he'd accept a gay Shakespeare hero?
Would she hide me in the back and stand by the door and say
anyone wants to get to him has to come through me?
Would she pray for me? Would he bless me?
Would he wash my body and cover me with flowers?
Would she admit me? Would he erase me?
Would you?

✳

The Westboro Baptist church have announced
that they will picket the funerals
of the Orlando victims shootings. "It's not about
that person. It's about that whole societal phenomenon"
said a spokesman, Steve Drain.
"It's never okay to be gay and it's never going to be okay
to be gay, no matter how much the spirit of the times
calls for the popularity of that sin," he added.

A couple who were killed in the Pulse nightclub attack
in Orlando hoped to get married within a short distance of the venue.
Today their families have announced that they will be buried side by side.

Despite widespread criticism the Westboro Baptist church have
announced that they are planning to protest at further funerals.

It's been happening and happening my whole life.
It will happen my whole life.

I take it your own business calls on you,
and you embrace the occasion to depart.

Pentimenti

It describes the repentance of painters,
how over time an image regretted
by its creator begins to emerge
through the layers of paint:
a stray limb or half-faced leer,
a chilled apple core on a plate.

Though could it not also describe ourselves,
the ones we let go of as we age,
those we try to obscure on dates
as we stare across the table, smiling.

I don't claim to know much about painting.
I once thought chiaroscuro was a cured meat.
But I do know regret, and a little of the soul,
it's repentant selves, how they wait.

After Pride

It isn't a fall, but a taking down,
a putting-away

the bare-chested men
who'd marched through town

have put on their t-shirts
and gone to the subway

hands in their pockets, sets of keys
gripped between their knuckles.

I've been there too: that carnival
of love and fear, that look

on the faces of passers-by,
the way a stare could mark you out

the way they'd tut and shield the eyes
of their kids. I remember face-paint,

how I scrubbed at my face, how I stared
at the rainbow in my hands

then back at my pale unrainbowed face;
and I remember my friend folding his flag,

so big at first it needed two to push
the ends together, how he folded it

and folded it until it was small enough
to fit into his bag, how afraid he was

that someone would want to look,
maybe his father, maybe a stranger on the train.

He called me at the weekend and told me
he'd chucked it away. He made some joke of it,

but even now I know he's folding it smaller,
that he hopes one day to find it gone.

Chechnya

You ask me why I fight, and I say it comes from ignorance.
I don't know what it is like to love unconditionally
or to forgive without bearing grudges. You can ask
any of my exes and they'll agree that I remember
transgressions like a wronged nation. And if you asked
them to describe me you'd learn that I'm a great maker
of incomplete lists, that I'm irrationally afraid of flying,
and that most days I prefer spending three hours alone.
There are many things I pretend to know that I don't
and many things I do not even slightly understand.

One of these things recently happened in Chechnya.
A 17 year old was thrown from a ninth floor balcony by his family
for being gay. There are many things about this I cannot know:
the impact of the body, how he split open upon impact,
the pattern he made on the pavement, the things that must
have skittered through his mind while falling nine floors, his terror,
the strength of his need to love in such a place, the depth
of his fear. Then there's his family, also unknowable, the uncle
who saw fit to leave his own home, to march across the small city,
to climb nine flights of stairs or to wait for an elevator to take him

to the door of his brother or sister, the passion and persuasiveness
of a speech that made that brother or sister decide to murder
their son. I cannot understand how someone could open the door
and then the next door to the balcony, could lift their son
like a struggling, begging piece of luggage and hurl him
out to the wide sky. I've known a little hatred but I can't figure this out,
this hate that rounds up men and takes them to camps, that beats
and breaks and kills, that is unreported and uninterrupted,
that brags it will eradicate gays by June.
I'd like to think that as he fell his murderers felt guilt,
that the mother fell to her wordless knees, that the father

screamed "what have I done!", that he had to be tackled by the uncle to not leap after his son. I'd like to think that this is what happened because this is my understanding of the human world, but in reality they probably didn't do these things. I cannot know what ran through their minds. What do their neighbours think of them? Are they seen as good citizens of Chechnya? Here's one more thing I pretend to know: that most people are good, that we can live in a society that is mostly accepting, that we can marry and adopt, and love. But there's also this deeper creeping knowledge: that some would have us crushed, that out there are millions who would wish us dead. This is why I fight.

The Plane

Lanzhou noodles in the underground mall
and, as the air is just *unhealthy for sensitive groups,*
we walk home through the skyscrapers of Huacheng park

and on towards the river, the Canton Tower beaming
like a neon chess queen, hawkers launching their toy helicopters
that spiral their slow arcs above us. We listen to the hammers

reverberating off the new twin towers of the IFC,
see the metal work-lift stuttering up its outside, the cranes
at the top hauling beams and glass and steel.

It's then, from nowhere, that I spot the plane: swooping in
over the shoulder of the river, flying low, much too low
and heading our way, wing-lights extinguished, a dark shadow

aimed like an arrow at us. I hate the world for filling me with fear,
my throat for its gasps, my heart's cowardice, my no-good legs.
I stood staring at the plane, a product of perfect submission

as it veered towards the buildings, steadied its trajectory
and approached the massive towers, then all at once burst
into song. "Look!" said my friend, "Look! Look at that!

The snow cranes are flying back home!"

IV – Lucky Cat

Happiness

Someone once told me
that the original carousel
was powered by a blind mule
eight feet down.

The more kids from the town demanded happiness
the harder the broken-backed beast lugged
its burden. And if it slowed for a breath
in its oubliette of dark, how quick the whip,
the kick of a boot.

I imagine that mule, its pit and circuitry,
the juddering cogs, fake stallions above,
their mouths set in a semblance of fierceness.

Happiness: I wonder if its riders
know or care how it works?

Talisman

I don't need an amulet
around my neck, don't need a jade bracelet

on my wrist, a twist of string, blessed
around my shin. I don't need onions

or jasmine above my door, don't need to live
on the eighth floor of this apartment complex,

could take the fourth bed on any ward
and not fear death. And I don't need the Lord

Buddha on my dashboard, nor a bible on the table
beside our bed, and I won't throw blind dice

at 3a.m. to test chance as if chance were a test.
And I don't need a lucky cat to lure you back

as if my life were a shop and my heart on sale,
as if the others who had rummaged through

the discount rails hadn't left
dry-washing their hands.

But what I need are your lectures on mess
and you laughing as I panic on flights

and your breath in the small hours
steadying the room, as the passengers above us

begin their descent, the captain requesting
the cabin crew be seated, releasing the airplane's wheels.

Guangzhou Daffodils

I wandered lonely on my way
to One Link Walk in Tianhe
past Huaxia Lu and Dongfeng Bei
and wondered briefly how you were.
I got into the shiny lift
and clocked on quickly for my shift.

I nipped out during that lunchtime
and walked among the tall skyscrapers
that stretch in their unending lines.
I paused at the window of a travel agents:
The Lake District, the rolling hills,
the graves, the golden daffodils.

The manager saw me standing there
and waved me in and sat me down.
I couldn't help but sit and stare
as the agent sold me my home town.
Five minutes in, I felt quite sure
and duly signed up for the tour.

For often sitting at my desk
in a vacant or a pensive mood
I need the snow, the hills, the risk
of falling, shortbread, solitude.
I'm all signed up, I'm on my way,
my plane is lifting through the grey.

The Coffin Path

I walk the three miles to Rydal
and watch red squirrels squabble in the trees
and after a mile I see a wake of buzzards
circling the high paths of the fell.

I sit on a stone where they used to rest the coffin
and dwell on those old sweating ghosts
on days like this, snow on the tops, snowdrops
pushing through, the bright white shock of apple blossoms.

It's then that the air leaks into the valley
and in a space between the sight and the sound
the snowdrops wilt, buzzards plunge from the sky,

squirrels topple and smash like pots, and I
grasp the frosted hand of a ghost, lift my coffin
and lead it through apple blossom, that falls like snow.

The Cairns

This morning we walked up the Lion and Lamb
and threw a small stone on the cairns.

We looked down on Heron Pike and Jackdaw Crag
as I explained what cairns were, how each rock

came from walkers who'd conquered the fell,
how they marked their ascent through these stones.

Then you told me about skyscrapers in China;
how workers etch a scratch on the metal beams,

how each floor they complete is redeemed on a tally,
achievement measured in meters of metal.

What is life if not these accumulations
the buildings and cairns seem to say.

A cloud rolled in along the top of Silver How
as I lifted my cairn stone away.

Sheepdogs in Shanghai

I see them on The Bund at nightfall,
threading their way through a tour group,
to their right the old bank, the stock exchange –
to their left The Huangpu, it's famous view.

Two of them stand on their hind legs and whine:
The Pearl Tower, The Bottle Opener, the river
crammed with boats, with noise and light,
Tibetan snowmelt that has made it to here.

Over time we lose track of who we are.
The water darkens, becomes undrinkable;
the dogs lose sight of their fields.
There's a deep need in us that we have left behind, so I speak

and the dogs look up at me; and though it's unthinkable
they'll know what I mean: *Away to me*, I breathe, *Come by*.

The Water Calligraphers

If I was content
I'd be like the men in Zhongshan Park
up and writing before the sun
armed with my bucket and brush.

Instead I'm late for work again,
not even pausing to watch
as men lift words from the water,
easing each stroke onto the flagstones

If I was content
I'd learn to write my poems with water.
The wind would lift them into the sky.
I wouldn't mind where they fell.